# L.A.T.T.

## LIFE AFTER TIK-TOK

THE TIK-TOK DOOR'S ARE "NOW" CLOSING...
AMERICA CAN FINALLY GET BACK TO NORMAL
AND AWAY FROM THE "CORPORATE
CLUTCHES" OF SOCIAL MEDIA AND TIK-TOK'S
ALGORITHMS AND THE

## "BUILD-A-BRAIN"

### SOCIAL MEDIA
#### TAKEOVER

# TIK "TIK" "TOK"

# BOooM!

#### WRITTEN BY
### IHAD TU TELLuM

# TABLE OF CONTENTS

OK, SO LET'S JUST GET THIS (BLANK) OUT THE WAY… IT HAS BECOME OBVIOUS THAT SOCIAL MEDIA SUCH AS FACEBOOK, INSTAGRAM, TWITTER (B.K.A) (X), AND TIK-TOK's, ALGORITHMS HAS BECOME, AN ENORMOUS MONEY GRAB AND A COMPLETE CORPORATE "LAUNCHING PAD" WITHOUT OUR GOVERNMENT GIVING US ANY EXPLANATION OF THE SOCIAL EFFECTS THAT HAS OCCURRED WITHIN OUR SOCIETY…

# L.A.T.T
## LIFE AFTER TIK-TOK

WRITTEN BY
IHAD TU TELLuM

CAN YOU OR WILL WE SURVIVE THE BIG-**3**

01-19-2025
THE TIK - TOK BAN WILL TAKE AFFECT HOWEVER, IT WILL BE TOTALLY UP TO THE U.S. SENATE AND CONGRESS TO OVERTURN OR POSSIBLY REVERSE, OR AMEND THE PROPOSED BAN ON TIK - TOK

# U.S. Copyright Office

## Library of Congress

## 101 Independence Avenue SE

## Washington, DC 20559-6000

## U.S. Copyright Office
## Receipt Case / SR#: 1-14440153041

## Case Date: 11/6/2024

## Title: L.A.T.T.  LIFE AFTER TIK-TOK

## Vol/Num/Issue:

## Materials Submitted:

## Quantity Format:

## ISBN:9798301903724

# INTRO:

**PLEASE NOTE:**
TO THE READER, L.A.T.T - HAS BEEN "SET-UP", AS A "REFERENCE GUIDE CONTAINING FACTUAL ARTICLES AND "INFORMATION" ... THIS GUIDE ALSO INCLUDES, OVER (120+) PAGES, FOCUSING ON THE IMPACT OF SOCIAL MEDIA, AND TOO ALSO BE USED AS A REFERENCE GUIDE FOR INFORMATIONAL PURPOSES, AND TO FACT CHECK THE TRUTH.

IT CAN (ALSO) BE USED AS (A) - BUFFER TO CONTROL THE SOCIAL MEDIA (BULLIES),,, TROLLS, AS WELL AS THE (OVER) "TWEAKED UNREGULATED" TIK-TOK ALGORITHMS.  L.A.T.T. LIFE AFTER TIK-TOK CAN POSSIBLY ELEVIATE SOME OF THAT UNWANTED BRAIN FATIGUE, (JUST JOKING:)


# L.A.T.T
## LIFE AFTER TIK-TOK

# AMERICA

THE TIK-TOK DOOR'S ARE "SOON" CLOSING... MERICA CAN FINALLY GET BACK TO NORMAL AND AWAY FROM THE "CORPORATE CLUTCHES" OF SOCIAL MEDIA AND TIK-TOK'S ALGORITHMS, THE

# "BUILD-A-BRAIN"
## SOCIAL MEDIA TAKEOVER

## L.A.T.T. LIFE AFTER TIK-TOK

This BOOK has a "F.A.F.O." Attitude with the approach towards the Social Media Conglomerates such as FACE BOOK, INSTAGRAM, SNAPCHAT, And TIK-TOK To give us the truth & answers, on their (Secretive, Manipulative and Harmful) Algorithms. As well As BYTE DANCE TIK-TOK Platform that has a "Cozy" Relationship with (Communist China) And why has America decided to Completely BAN TIK-TOK On 01/19/2025 while America waits for the truth and the unknown.

## ABOUT THE AUTHOR:

Ihad Tu Tellum resides in the Chicago area, Mr. Tellum has served Honorably in the United States Navy for over Ten years active Duty during the start of the (Iran-Iraq Hostage Crisis): Mr. Tellum is currently retired and A Disabled (Vet) and –- an Up-and-coming Writer and Entrepreneur and has been Unapologetic in his approach and his Life's Journey. And this is what has been demonstrated, in terms of His attempt to address the implications and the internal impacts of Social Media.

L.A.T.T. LIFE AFTER TIK-TOK, has been formatted (Mostly) as a Reference and Personal Information Guide, to attempt and to address the "Over Tweaked" Unregulated Social Media Conglomerates such as (Facebook, YouTube, and TIK-TOK's Algorithms and Small Screen Technology, that has been a complete onslaught from the Use of Social Media on our Society, without having a thorough explanation.

L.A.T.T. LIFE AFTER TIK-TOK, has allowed the writer to put his Own Voice as well as his Message and Perspective and Opinion on this "Urgent" and Necessary Subject Matter, that seems to have been (Avoided): A Subject

Matter, that (Nearly) everyone seem to have tried, their (Best) to Avoid, In having a Conversation about  (Social Media) and their Unregulated Policies, that has been Unleashed into our Society.  L.A.T.T.  LIFE AFTER TIK-TOK, Is the latest Message and Opinion, that is Honest, and Open to the Reader that is based on his own personal challenges with his Own Family and the impact of Social Media, and the Unanswered Response from the Social Media Corporations, of the effects from the use of Targeted Algorithms on various Platforms towards its users.

In closing, L.A.T.T. LIFE AFTER TIK-TOK, has been presented with "Factual Research" of Various articles and information, With a (Fact-Checked) Style Format that provides more of a relevant and clear Approach, that is based strictly on the Subject Matter, so that you can (Avoid) the Typical "Lecture - ristic Style Format"  (Leaving the Reader) still Unsure and Confused of what they Just read about Social Media); L.A.T.T.  Provides actual information as well as Researched Articles from Professional Writers and Personal information within the (Space) of Social Media and what the Effects and Impact has been from the Usage.

## L.A.T.T. LIFE AFTER TIK-TOK:

Soooo, I GUESS YOU MAY (WANNA) "GO" GRAB YOU SOME POPCORN:)

To WHOM IT MAY CONCERN... Yes, To Whom It May Concern, is a "Perfect" way to start off this particular (Subject), for the Sometimes "OVER EXHAUSTED" (F.O.M.O) "SCROLL-A-HOLIC"

Or the Typical Social Media User, Or if You or someone you know fits this description then continue reading: L.A.T.T. LIFE AFTER TIK-TOK

Or Unless, "YOU", are still in Deep Denial, Or saying that You have not been affected by Social Media Or (Don't) know of anyone that hasn't been affected by the Latest Social Media Craze, that has literally Consumed the Entire Planet as we know it.

And if, L.A.T.T. (Doesn't Fit) Your Desired Reading Consumption, then I would "Advise" and Strongly Suggest that you should "Discontinue Reading" this Information, especially if you or anyone you Know,

"Hasn't" been affected by Social Media then I would fully Understand.

So, If this is the case let's take a Brief moment and (Honestly); Take a look back over the past (50) + Years, and allow yourself to reflect on how the world has (Evolved),  as well as, changed In terms of Communication on Our (Basic) way of life when it comes to our (Overall) Socialization skills that seems to have Dwindled amongst each other, and how certain individuals have come to the "Lack" of (Basic) interaction towards each other, it also appears to have been a drastic change in today's relationships, Within Our Families, and Our Children from the sudden impact of Social Media.

Even towards Our daily work habits and social skills amongst each other, to say the least.  We must also look at and consider how "Narrow" our Personal, and Social behavior appears to have become extremely "(Self Isolated)" for several hours a day with a (Selfish) "Taught-Like"  - "Regimented Styled

Daily Assignment" that the average person consumes and focuses on Social Media throughout the Day comfortably, Unaware and Unconsciously attached to a pre-occupied Schedule on "Their Phones, along with other Digital Devices or Video Games that has completely occupied their entire day for the most part, rather than spending quality time with Friends and Family, or even School or Work.  And when you take a serious look at it, even our Inner-Actions, towards each other have been restructured (As if we did it too Ourselves)...To a Point that appears, as if we have "Self-Download" Our-self into a (Fre#aKn) "Human App"  Or have been, Simply (Merged) together Like a Marriage of a "Bride & Groom" that has been attached and (Bolted) to a (Algorithmic) Altar of Various Social Media Platforms like TIK-TOK.

And to be completely Honest, it feels as if Social Media has "Self - Re-Rooted" itself into our Daily lives, "Culinary Style" (almost) as if it came from a "CORPORATE SOCIAL MEDIA RECIPE" and Served to us on a "Silver

Platter". So, if this is the case, let's be "Perfectly Clear" …

And If you still Appear to Be, One of the Ones, that May Have a Subtle case, or a Diagnosis of "TIK-TOK Denial Syndrome", Then I suggest that You:

"NEED TO BLINK TWICE" And Buckle Up:

SPOILER ALERT TO THE DAILY SOCIAL MEDIA SCROLL-A-HOLICS:

TIC-TOK IS OWNED BY THE "BYTE DANCE" CORPORATION, THAT IS ASSOCIATED WITH AND CONTROLLED BY COMMUNIST CHINA, TIK-TOK HAS BEEN GIVEN A WARNING TO DISBAND AND DIS-ASSOCIATE THEIR TIES WITH CHINA OR THEY WILL BE "BANNED" ON JANUARY 19, 2025:

SO, THIS IS FOR THE TIK-TOK HEADS, YOU'VE BEEN OFFICIALLY WARNED:

# LIFE AFTER TIK-TOK

CAN YOU OR WILL WE SURVIVE THE BIG-3

# CHAPTER ONE

"1974-2024"
## LIKE IT NEVER EVEN HAPPENED:

Well let us Slowly begin or attempt to figure out what has happened to us as a Society, in terms of how we interact, communicate, and how technology has changed the world over the past 50+ years.

Technology has had a chance to improve over the years, and how it has impacted our daily lives and the advancement in various fields, Such as in Space, Manufacturing, Farming, and also in Education to name a few.

Technology has also been used and has enhanced us into our current future at a somewhat casual pace, (But) in some cases it has accelerated and advanced a Little-Bit too quickly, that seems to have changed how certain Companies and Corporations have used their Technology, not to help Us, but has been only used for their Personal and Financial Gain "Like-a-Elon Musk Style" along with the Billion Dollar Chinese Corporation (ByteDance), the Owners of TIK-TOK.

And Now, with the influx of Social Media it appears to have altered our Relationships towards our Own Personal Freedom along with Friends, Families, as well as, even how Parents Raise and Teach their Children Basic Social Skills on a daily basis and as of Now it seems that we have fully lost Control of what we See, Hear, or Watch, or even Taught, when it Comes to Our Daily Consumption.

Social Media has also changed Social Economics as we know it, and with the rapid change in Today's Corporate Technology, Like YouTube, Facebook, Instagram and TIK-TOK, has been allowed to "Run Rampant" and unregulated throughout our Society almost (Seamlessly) that has created a "Digital Island" of Separation, and (or) a (Buffer) towards our Family, especially when it involves Social Media's (Uncontrollable) Consumption, on a Hourly and Daily basis that has been Dominated by Social Media.

It also seems to have changed as well as Challenged Our Families into becoming more "Un-Traditionalized" along with a (Blurred) Uninsured and Unsecured focus of Obtaining Truthful and Factual Information).

And even Now the Average (Social Media User) will even "Self Verify" their Own Friends and Family's information, and will Even Question them, and will Give them a (Side-Eye) response, (Especially) if they didn't hear it from a Social Media Platform or from their Isolated Group Chat First.

It Seems that today's Society when it comes to using certain Platforms like (Facebook, Snap, Instagram, YouTube and TIK-TOK, In which it seems to have Developed, and Put in Place an "Anti - Trust Theory" amongst ourselves and the Average Social Media User, that seems to have erased our basic "Critical Thinking Skills" Or even (The) use of a Reliable Cognitive Format like S.T.A.R. Situation-Task-Action-Result, when it comes to Communication and Trust between each other has been Socially Diminished.  What needs to Happen, is that AMERICA Should be Given the Corporations Like TIK-TOK And FACEBOOK The (Side-Eye) Response, for All the Unanswered questions Of the Non-Regulations on Social Media.

Even Now, with the Rapid and "Expressed" Production of Today's Technology and Information that we consume, Is (Clearly) Unregulated, and for the most part the information hasn't even been "Fact Checked" from the various Social Media Platforms, that have been allowed to endlessly (Spread) "Untrue Information" throughout our Daily Lives:

And to be Completely 100% To the Reader, is that the Social Media's impact seems to have - Allegedly Inserted a, "Flawed Ingredient" into the social Media's Platform that has Literally (Wreaked - Havoc) Overall within our Society. And the Corporation have yet to fully explain to the Public and Our Society's deterioration and Social Residue, that seems to have left the Mental and Psychological effects of Social Media, and how it has become SOCIALLY TOXIC:

This alone with the Distribution of the (Over-Selfish) and (Over Opinionated) and sometimes (Hateful) responses towards each other Just to Prove a Point, and to push the So-Called (Negative Energy) just so they can continuously "Spoon-Feed" the Mindless Trolls, and their follower's information of what they want them to hear (Even) if the Facts and Information is (True Or Not).

And even now, If you Just take a Brief Look at Today's Typical "Social Media "Snobbish/Social Media User", with their (Selfish attacks towards Each Other) and their Personal Indulgence, along with The "Must Have" (Overly Priced) I-Phone, or Android Device seems to be in their Own World.

Just take a look online or on (Facebook or Instagram) of the Constant Small Screen Technology that is "Fueled" from TIK-TOK's,

(DTC) Direct to Consumer Approach, just So that they can brandish their Own Self Branded Publishing of their "Endless and (Self-A-Fyed) Personal Catalog" of personal "Selfies" with their New (I-Phone #16 or Android) as they Proudly "Hoist" and Share Their New (Digital Gadgets) amongst their Online "FAM - CLUB".

Ok, So let's just take a Quick "Pause" and give them a moment, (I guess), LET'S Applaud Them:

## As they celebrate, their (Self Accomplishment) with their new

# "Digital Trophy"

As they strategically "Flaunt" their (Self Gratification) of Accomplishments amongst their New Collection of their (Isolated Group of So-called) Friends and Random "SCROLL-A-HOLICS" on the various Social Media Platforms.

While the "Fact-less" Social Media (Feeds) and (Catchy Ads) are continuously Distributed, as they share their endless (Rants and Cartoonish) unemotionally (Gifs) of emojis amongst each other with (Untrue and Unfiltered) so-called facts.

And if you noticed this type of Behavior from some of your friends and family, with the recent "Off the Cuff Type of Social Activity" this alone, has "Severely Severed" our way of thinking as well as caused more of a (Division or a Social Gap of a Selfish Isolation) Amongst each other, (*Rather than Bringing Us Closer Together) with a Healthy Sensible and Positive (Outcome and Solution)*.

Please Note: If this does not fit Your "Personal Identity" Please Disregard:

And Please, Please, Please, Just to let you Know that you (Probably) will be "Banished" if you are (Caught) Amongst your So-Called "Iphone Friends" when they find out that you are still using an Android Phone. "Just saying" you gotta be safe in these (Social Media) Streets…(Just Joking:)

Meanwhile, At the (BIG-3's Social Media) "Digital Algorithm Ranch" … The "BIG-3" are in a Horrific (Overdrive Mode), and they are Currently, And are "Massively Over-Tweaking the "F#CK" Out of their Corporate Algorithms, with Companies like (TIK-TOK), FACEBOOK, and INSTAGRAM, that seems to have an endless supply of the Best "BUILD-A-BRAIN" Algorithmic Tools, that's on today's Market, (That's awaiting to Be) Strategically Shoved Into Our Brains.

With the Best Technology that Money can Buy with their "Glorified Technicians" as they "Sit Perched" inside their Lavish "Tech-ed Out" Billion Dollar Campus, Just to be at (BYTE-DANCE, Beck and Call) Waiting to assist in TIK-TOK's Research & Development Department.

Hell, I bet that they even have a Separate Room. Just for their Money Counting

Machines, and the Back Room "I Bet" is Probably (Draped With) Customized Wallpaper of Hundreds and Hundreds of Dollar Bills including Chinese Yen as they Build their addictive Algorithms that would eventually be inserted into their New Apps.

Even now It seems that they are so "(F#kN Diabolical)" when it comes to the impact and effects from Social Media, is that the (BIG-3) Social Media Platform Has had a (Limited) response and  a somewhat (Muted) answer from the Social Media Corporations as they continue to keep Things "Hush-Hush" and (Under-Wraps and Under-Funded) when it comes to their Overall Budget   on what is spent towards the Overall effects from Social Media.

With this alone it also appears that the (BIG-3) Social Media Corporations seems to have Orchestrated a "Perfect Pitch" Amongst each Other, Of a Complete (Silent) "Symphonic" and "Colluded" Tone, that seems to have been "Stitched" together, (Between) the BIG-

3'S, Corporate, with an (Unrecognizable Fabric) a Fabric that has not disclosed their Hidden Agendas.

That features a Host of unfiltered Algorithms that has been (ALLOWED) To be Distributed across Today's Social Media Platforms, that seems to have been Directly filtered into our Society.

With Distractive Algorithms along with a continuous (Spew) of "Un-regulatory Content" that has (Endlessly Flooded) our Traditional Social Narrative, while the BIG-3 - Collect Billions and Billions in Profits, through their Social Media Platforms. It appears that it has formed a "DIGITAL- HIGH LIKE - ADDICTION"

That seems to have been "VISUALLY INHALLED", Along with an Over saturation, of a (Added Algorithmic, TIK-TOK Like Boost) of "Subliminal and Thirsty Ads" that has been attached and Designed from "Generations and Generations of  a – Strategically (Self Approved Selection of Professionally Timed

Format), Of an Undisclosed form of "Small Screen Technology" of "Slick & Click-ish Ads" With an Enhanced Frequency, to further increase profits without providing any regulations or limitations of (Viewership Consumption) or Give any (Valid) answers or "Warning Labels" of Potential Damages to Our Society Including the Consumption and Usage too our Children both Physically or Mentally.

**PLEASE NOTE: L.A.T.T - HAS BEEN SET-UP AS A "REFERENCE" AND "INFORMATION GUIDE", THAT FOCUSES ON THE IMPACT OF SOCIAL MEDIA...**

**TIC-TOK IS OWNED BY THE "BYTE DANCE" CORPORATION, THAT IS ASSOCIATED WITH AND PRESENTLY CONTROLLED BY COMMUNIST CHINA, TIK-TOK HAS BEEN GIVEN A WARNING TO DISBAND AND DIS-ASSOCIATE THEIR TIES WITH CHINA OR THEY WILL BE "BANNED" ON JANUARY 19, 2025:**

Now, Let's just take a (Quick) Peek at the acceleration of how Far and how Fast we have advanced our Technology in the Past (50+) years both Good and Bad, With Social Media:

#1. The first Toshiba Floppy Disk Drive was introduced in 1974.

#2. 1974, President NIXON was forced "OUT", and had to (Resigns from Office), And President Gerald Ford was In after Nixon was forced to Resign, following the Watergate Scandal, and believe me if (Nixon) have had the Use and access of Social Media and foreign influence, I bet he would have used it.

Unfortunately, President Ford Only lasted (895 Days) as the United States President. AND DID NOT USE FAKE BOTS OR FAKE NEWS FROM RUSSIA, OR FAKE INFORMATION LIKE THE SOCIAL MEDIA TACTICS USED BY THE (PREVIOUS) ADMINISTRATION, THAT MAY HAVE BEEN USED TO ATTEMPT TO "STEAL" OR ALTER THE LAST OR CURRENT

ELECTION WITH THE CONSTANT INFLUX OF FAKE ADS FROM COMMUNIST COUNTRIES.

#3. ROE V. WADE (1974) Was the Law of the Land which a landmark decision of the US Supreme Court ruled that the Constitution of the United States protected (WOMEN) With the right to have an abortion.

#4. *The Rumble in the Jungle: Muhammad Ali and George Foreman fought in a boxing match in Zaire, nicknamed "The Rumble in the Jungle" One of the Worlds Biggest Fights without Social Media...*

#5. Hank Aaron Broke Babe Ruth's Career home-run record while playing for the Atlanta Braves on April 8, 1974. Hank Aaron Became a National "Baseball Icon" and a Household Legend. And Once Again Without the use of (Social Media) *And the entire World both Domestically and Internationally, was able to "Communicate to the Masses without the use of Social Media.*

#6. The number (One# Song) of 1974 was "The Way We Were" by Barbra Streisand. In which I Belive was a "Perfect" Title for a Song in Our Lives to Remember how Normal life was… (Prior) to the Social Media Craze.

 #7. Tandem Computers was founded in 1974.

#8. The Top Movie in 1974 was, The Exorcist, The Sting, The Great Gatsby, The Poseidon Adventure, and Godfather Part II. That was (Viewed) and made Millions and Millions of Dollars at the "BOX OFFICE" without today's Advanced Streaming Technology.

#9. And in (1978) The first commercially released (VHS) VCR, was released to the public (Even) though the first (VCR) Original Design was developed and introduced in (1956).

#10.  And in1979, Technology introduced The Original Sony Walkman TPS-L2, on July 1, 1979.

We must also consider that America has always been curiously "Tinkering" and focused when it comes to advancing technology.  In 1945 believe it or not the *first Microwave Oven was invented.*

According to the American Physical Society, The Self-taught Engineer Percy Spencer (Filed the first Patent for the Microwave Oven in 1945.

And in 1946: The first commercial microwave —the RadaRange— was sold by Raytheon to restaurants, large canteens and ships' galleys. It was nearly six feet tall, weighed more than 750 pounds, used about 3,000 watts of power and sold for roughly $5,000.

And it wasn't until (21-Years) Later in (1967) when the first Microwave Oven Finally was presented to the General Public, and Finally came to the Market. And by (1972), the (Litton Atherton) Division, Minneapolis, introduced new microwave ovens, to the public that were priced at $349 and $399, to tap into the market estimated at $750 million, and by 1976, according to Robert I Bruder, President of the

Division. While prices remained high, new features continued to be added to home models. And to add my (Humble Opinion), After the invention of the Microwave Oven, it seems to have (Sped) Up Americas Society that seem to have Sparked our Curiosity and (Technical Vision) as well as our Sense of Obtaining the – "I WANT IT NOW" Mentality.

I would like to further introduce information and the Impact of Social Media that has been discussed in the earlier years (In that) we were Warned...

## Disruption By:

# Louis Wirth:

**Former President of international Sociological Association**

"Louis Wirth" and The "American Journal" (Sourced in 1938), for example, wrote about consequences of a rapid rural urban transition for modes of life, including declines in kinship bonds, neighborliness, and personal acquaintanceship, and substitution of secondary for primary

Societies. Sociological analyses suggested that "mass society" entails a general reduction in the number of communal relationships, together with diminished functionality for those that remain; such atomization, it was feared, would render large numbers of people open to manipulation by elites and susceptible to mass appeals (Kornhauser, 1968). Wellman (1979) terms these "Communities lost" perspectives.

Many mid-20th century empirical studies suggested that informal social ties. A substantial minority of the relationships were potential sources of everyday and emergency assistance (Wellman, 1979). These studies and others like them demonstrated that informal social ties had hardly vanished, notwithstanding the considerable macroscopic changes thought to have threatened them. While less focused on the spatial aspect of "community" than earlier work, more recent discussions of downward trends in "social capital" raised parallel worries about declining social integration. Informal interpersonal ties are, of course, only one aspect of this multifaceted concept which can also encompass connections to voluntary groups, social trust, and civic engagement, among other things.

END

And in a more recent article, when it comes to the effects of (Social Media) Peter V. Marsden and Sameer B. Srivastava November 6, 2011, In their Article discussed Social Trends in the United States, 1972-2000s: Evidence from the General Social Survey, edited by Peter V. Marsden. Princeton University Press.

Analysts and commentators periodically raise the prospect that large-scale social changes might substantially alter patterns of interpersonal relations, often for the worse. Among putative sources of such disruptions to the social fabric are industrialization, urbanization and the development and expansion of mass media.

It is also stated that general reduction in the number of communal relationships, together with diminished functionality for those that remain; such atomization, it was feared, would render large numbers of people open to manipulation by elites and susceptible to mass appeals (Kornhauser, 1968).

Wellman (1979) terms these "Communities lost" perspectives. Many mid-20th century empirical studies suggested that informal social ties, a substantial minority of relationships, were potential sources of everyday and emergency assistance (Wellman, 1979). These studies and others like them demonstrated that informal social ties had hardly vanished, notwithstanding the considerable macroscopic changes thought to have threatened them.

"Putnam's (2000: p. 115)" asserts that there has been "a striking diminution of regular contacts with our friends and neighbors." He cites several factors as contributors to reduced connectedness, changing family and household structures; suburbanization, residential mobility and spatial dispersion; electronic entertainment, especially television; and the replacement of a highly Civic cohort born before 1940 by Baby Boomers and Generation X.

In comparing two (GSS) samples separated by about 20 years. McPherson, Smith Lovin and Brashears (2006) reported a particularly dramatic fall in the number of confiding relationships available to U.S. adults, from a 1985 average of 3.0 to a 2004 figure of 2.1; an estimated 22.6% of the 2004 sample reported no such confidant, compared to 8.0% in 1985—indicating an appreciable rise in isolation.

*This Information states that, In an age where digital devices are ubiquitous, the dynamics of family conversations have been reshaped.*

The traditional model of direct, in-person interactions, often characterized by immediate emotional responses and physical presence, is increasingly complemented - and at times, replaced - by digital exchanges.

## L.A.T.T.
## LIFE AFTER TIK-TOK

At this Point Life After Tik-Tok, Can justify that our Society was not "Originally Prepared" or (Intelligently) Set up, to be "Digitally Obstructed", and just Simply "Hoarded" Away like "Mindless Sheep" that has basically left us to (Graze) in a Digital "Algorithmic Maze", Or for us to figure this "S%@t" Out Ourselves. (OR A MOVE AND GET OUT THE WAY) Mentality from the Likes of a Quote from the (Rapper Ludacris). Or just jump –On Board– with a "One Way

Corporate Social Media Ticket" or just (Patiently) wait on the sideline just to see whatever they "Gonna" Develop next.

And  I Really, Really, Really, don't think that America was ready to separate or exchange its (Traditional Values) in Exchange with this Unexplained, "Corporate Driven Super Advanced Modern Society", in which most of Society has Literally been left to (Play Catch-Up) to this More, (Modern and Technical Tradition) that seems to be the Reason Family Values have been Separated by Social Media Today.

And now it appears that we have been unable to adapt in most cases, to even explain or give a valid answer on what will happen next, with our present family structure or our daily functionality to even attempt to restructure ourselves (Back) to our Original and Traditional Family Values, Or have any future plans or Answers from Corporate America on how to put the "Genie Back In the Bottle"

Social Media Corporations (Has Yet) to provide the necessary (Tool-Kit) or any Written or Verbal instructions or explanation on how to fix our lives and put our Original lives back together again, (Just so that we could move Forward) from the current unrecognized and the unknowns of what is going to happen next.

And in this case, It will have to be a (Astronomical) and a "Pivotal Leap" for Society to Continually be able to "Grasp" Or Afford the Cost of New Technology (Prior) to us being able to fully understand or keep Caught Up from the accelerated adjustment of the latest upgrades of technology.

And with a Recent Quote about Social Media that I recently heard while Watching CNBC, On T.V.

A quote by: Brian Schwalb, Attorney General of the District of Columbia, and (1 of 14)

States that are in the process of filling a (Law-Suit) against "Tik-TOk, - and said that,

TIK-TOK "IS LIKE A DIGITAL NICOTINE" END QUOTE:

I would like to also offer (My Own Quote) By Ihad Tu Tellum "TIK-TOK" SHOULD BE CONSIDERED "DIGITAL MALPRACTICE" AND CHARGED WITH DISTRIBUTION OF "DIGITAL CRACK-LIKE" CONSUMPTION.

Please Note: This Historical data was used for Reference Purposes Only; the information has Been Fact Checked and includes freedom of speech and to (By-Pass) the Trolls Unfocused Commentary on this Particular Subject Matter:

PANDORA'S "BILLION DOLLAR CORPORATE BOX" AND THE (FCC) GOVERNMENT AGENCY IS NOW FINALLY OPEN FOR BUSINESS, TO THE SOCIAL MEDIA CORPORATIONS... "YEEEEAH"

# CHAPTER TWO
## RIGHT BEFORE OUR EYES

Soooo, if I can be allowed to elaborate and go (*further*) into The Social Media Craze, It seems "Allegedly" that this particular subject has been (Simply) By-passed or Overlooked by the Medical and Psychological Society for the most part in giving a definition of why have Social Media been allowed to go Unanswered by the Social Media Corporations on their algorithms.

"SO, NOT TO LET THEM OFF THE PERVERBALLY HOOK" It appears "Allegedly" that the Medical and Psychological Society, in general has (Not been as Vocal) and somewhat (Impotent-ly and Ineffective) when it came to Sounding the Alarm, or even "Hitting the Brakes" to Warn Parents and Regular Daily Social Media Users of Any Potential Effects from Using Social Media Or to Obtain or seek financial information (If Any) on what Social Media

Companies Spend on the Harmful Effects that may be caused from the use of Social Media.

In which I find it amazing and somewhat appalling, to not even suggest or make an (Applicable Warning) label for the users. Like the label, that was Designed and Placed On a (Pack Of Cigarettes) After the (BILLION) Dollar Lawsuit from Millions of People that Allegedly "Died from using their Product or Obtained and Unknown Illnesses" (and Or) alleged illness from the Direct use of their Tobacco Products.

Or (Maybe), That... The "BIG-3" (Allegedly) Gave the Medical Board "Not saying they did anything Wrong" the "(NO LOOK CASH... I-MEAN-PASS)" that has (seemingly) given them the Virtual "Green Light" to the (BIG-3) Social Media Corporations. Or did the Medical Board (Possibly) Mistaken or "Under Evaluated" the Under-Lying, (Symptoms) that Social Media's Corporate America, (A.K.A THE BIG-3) didn't want the (Symptoms) to be (*Revealed*) and that it may just become

Potentially, "Infectious" from the Over usage of Social Media. (Both) Medically and Psychologically (*Disruptive*) when it was Introduced to Our Society, from the unregulated Usage of the (BIG-3's) Social Media Product. Similar to the "Tobacco Companies alleged Potential Harms" from their Products.

It appears that, Social Media was Finally Summoned Before the United States Congress:

And what was inappropriate for the most part was that the (BIG-3), well at least (One-Of-Them), that was Interviewed By the (UNITED STATES CONGRESS) And This is what I got while Watching this (event) On the News:

Is that Trump's "New" (Primary Puppeteer) MARK ZUCKERBERG, Openly Displayed a "VENTRILOQUIST(IC)" Type of Display. Right in front of the United States Congress, In Which allowed ZUCKERBERG, who (seemly) enabled himself to Talk, Out Of *(Both)* The

(FRONT and the SIDE of His NECK) ... This alone, was a Complete "Visual and 'Viral' Feat", That has (NEVER) Been (Openly) SEEN, HEARD, Or PERFORMED IN FRONT OF A (SITTING) AUDIENCE, (BUT), Only (a) ZUCKERBERG Was Able to "Pull-It-Off" this Level of an (Academy Award) Performance:

As ZUCKERBERG gave His "WATERED DOWN" Version and told the United States Congress that Social Media Was Virtually Harmless.

As ZUCKERBERG, (Sheepishly) Sat in the (Halls Of Congress) in the "COMFY" "Overstuffed" Leather Chairs, as he Calmly Sat (Perfectly) "Perched" with his "Thin-Lipped" Calculated, and Articulated "Rehearsed" responses, as He "Slowly Sipped" His Water, Like -a- "Hummingbird" from the "Government Issued" (GI) Bottled Water.

Zuckerberg seems to have had a noticeable (Facial) expression and Frown, from the

(Unfamiliar Taste of the Government Issued Water), that was far-from the "Bougie" Brands of Water that ZUCKERBERG was accustomed to. As he Politely (Unleashed) the Ultimate Social Media Platforms, as being completely Innocent of any wrongdoing, to the (United States Congress) and the General Public (Without) even Blinking an Eye.

Nor did Zuckerberg offer or Give any Solutions or a Cure, or a Possible Diagnosis or WARNING, as ZUCKERBERG proceeded with His Dialogue to the United States Congress, with His "SCALPEL(ED)" Like Tongue as, ZUCKERBERG (Allegedly) and Methodically, continued effortlessly removing all of the remaining "Political Hurdles" and "Obstacles" as the United States Congress remained (In Awe) with a seemingly Clueless response.

As ZUCKERBERG continued, and was able to Tactfully Maneuver, literally, un-touched in front of the (UNITED STATES CONGRESS) with an (Oblique and Verbal) shift that allowed Him to Sprint out of the (Halls Of Congress) like an Olympic (100 meter relay) Track Star, directly to the "GREEDY-3's" Financial Destinations and to his Offshore Accounts, Off the Backs of the American People.

## Or Should we just have Believed what The "BIG-3" Told Us...

Please Note: This Historical data was used for Reference Purposes Only that has Been Fact Checked, and it also includes freedom of speech and to (By-Pass) the Trolls Unfocused Commentary on this Particular Subject Matter:

TIC-TOK IS OWNED BY THE "BYTE DANCE" CORPORATION, THAT IS ASSOCIATED WITH AND PRESENTLY CONTROLLED BY COMMUNIST CHINA, TIK-TOK HAS BEEN GIVEN A WARNING TO DISBAND AND DIS-ASSOCIATE THEIR TIES WITH CHINA OR THEY WILL BE "BANNED" ON JANUARY 19, 2025:

# CHAPTER THREE

## TIK-TOK'S - BUILD-A-BRAIN TAKEOVER

Therefore, at this point I Hope you Have "considered" the Information of the Original and Personal Reference and Prospective Provided in this Information Guide:

So Let Me Attempt to Provide the Reader with a (Virtual) "**AIR-QUOTE**" And to continue with an Adult Conversation or to engage, into the "Light Blinking" Phenom, called the "BIG-3" and the Social Media Craze, as it relates to the possible Truth and or the Solution to the (WHO, WHAT, WHEN, WHERE & HOW):

Social Media for the most part have (Been) abruptly, Introduced, and Generally came upon - Us, (Un-announced), and has Only shown a "Flicker" of (Un-Bashfulness), that Has become a "Virtual Love and Hate Relationship" into our Society without any explanation or remorse of the "Impregnated" Mental feelings and Psychological feelings that has been introduced un-announced

"Algorithmically" that you may have experienced from Social Media.

And What i'm basically saying is that (Originally) Social Media seems to have gradually come into our existence without us asking Or being (FOREWARNED) Of the Introduction of Social Media. (If you can just Understand what I'm Saying) ...

We didn't know, or (Just), Sat around and requested it or Ordered (Social Media) Like Ordering Pizza, or a Gourmet Burger, (Hell)' We didn't even know that (Social Media was even a Thing) With various Platforms Like Instagram, TIK-TOK - Or even what an (Algorithm) was Until Social Media was actually HERE.

We also didn't know if we would even need Social Media, or how it would work AND NOW, (All of a Sudden) it appears that we "Can't Function Without It. "OK SO WHAT HAPPENED WAS":)

The Next thing that we realized was, That, (Social Media had "Slowly Crept In, User By, User By - User, and Abruptly Introduced" itself into Our Society.

Social Media was also (Heavily) sponsored by the "Big-3" Corporations, without any formal explanation (Or) Even with a Proper Introduction,of what it would eventually become, Or if there would be any effects that may occur from the Over usage,or would have any lingering effects from the use of Social Media Algorithms, and we should be furthered "Stunned" of the Lack of Information.

Social Media Now appears, almost like, a "Nosey Neighbor" that Collects and Gathers "All" of Your Personal Data, Your Locations, and all your Purchases, and (Then) smothers you with endless Notifications and Ads, and alerts throughout your Entire Day.

You can also look at Social Media as a "House Guest", that has overstayed their welcome. And then if you're not watching - (Social

Media will turn around and ask (YOU) Do you Have a Problem with (US) Collecting and Asking you for All Your Personal Data and then would "Rudely" Ask you – "DIDN'T YOU READ THE (50 PAGES) OF FINE PRINT".

The "Big-3" Social Media Platforms seems to have been given permission to Live "RENT FREE" in Our Head, Our Body and Our "DIGITAL SOUL".

Even with our Kids and Family, With an, "O'h By the Way" nonchalant attitude when they tell you to (Hit) the (Autosign), of the (Hypothetical 27 Page Contract) that they Know you didn't Read, while they continue Gathering and Concealing all your Personal Data for their use of research and continuing not to explain the overall effects...

And here is another article that further explains various Social Media Platforms and Algorithms:

*Importing big tech regulation by an anonymous Writer:*

*Social media companies aren't as forthright as they could be about how their platforms work. We know social media has fundamentally impacted politics and our health. So, what's the government doing about social media? That's been the trillion-dollar question, specifically in the United States.*

*Top executives across Meta, Twitter, TikTok, YouTube, and Snap have all been grilled on Capitol Hill. Facebook whistleblower Frances Haugen appeared before Congress last year stating that "the severity of this crisis demands that we break out of our previous regulatory frames."Lawmakers have introduced bills here and there that try to take on such issues as addictive algorithms and surveillance advertising. But so far, no meaningful regulation has taken shape— unlike in the European Union, which has introduced legislation including the General Data Protection Regulation and Digital*

*Services Act aimed at enforcing transparency from big tech and protecting users' privacy. Rebekah Tromble, director of the Institute for Data, Democracy, and Politics at George Washington University, believes the same hasn't been done in the U.S. because of interpretations of the First Amendment and increasing political polarization. "It's hard to see our way out of this. If there's any real hope, it will be Europe that's leading the way," Tromble says. "The European regulation that's in the pipeline is going to have an impact far beyond Europe. Those studies and audits that the platforms are going to have to open themselves up to, they'll be focused on the impacts on European citizens, but we'll be able to say a lot about what the likely impacts are on American citizens. So, there, I do have a bit of optimism," As she Continues. "But In terms of how we might wrest the public's power back" and achieve fundamental accountability for the platforms in the U.S., "I remain unfortunately pretty pessimistic overall."*

*What researchers like Tromble and Joshua Tucker, co-director of NYU's Center for Social Media and Politics, are after is access to ethically sourced user data. "Access is like the prime mover of this, because I can't tell you what the regulation should look like if I don't know what's actually happening on the platforms," Tucker says. "The only way that those of us who don't work for the platforms are gonna know what's happening on the platforms is if we have access to the data and if we can run the kinds of studies that we need to run to be able to try to get answers to these questions."*

*END*

# L.A.T.T
## LIFE AFTER TIK-TOK

## AMERICA

**TIK-TOK DOORS ARE CLOSING SOON
AND NOW IS THE TIME TO GET BACK TO
NORMAL AND AWAY FROM THE "ALGORITHMIC
CLUTCHES" OF SOCIAL MEDIA AND TIK-TOK's**
## BUILD-A-BRAIN
### TAKEOVER

If you look at the Introduction of Social Media, it has basically gone (UN-CHECKED) as well as Completely (Under Regulated) into our daily lives.

And over the Past Years (Social Media) and The "(BIG-3)" has been capable, for over the past (15 +) Years, seems to have been giving an unprotected (Like) "Condom-Free" type, of Access and (a) Virtual "Unlimited Permission Slip" by the (Federal Government) and the (FCC). The U.S. Government also appears to have allowed the Social Media Corporations, to slowly Inject and administer a structured, and Unregulated Digital format into our Society.

The (BIG-3) and Social Media has even (Allowed) Foreign Companies from Various Countries and Corporations like *"BYTE DANCE"* The TIK-TOK" - Corporation Out Of China, and even (Russia's Putin); has made several attempts to "CLOG" America's Airways with untrue, Unchecked, "Filthy Political-Trash(y) Un-checked Media Ads" that were allowed to (Alledley) participate in Our last Election, Just like Before, as if they were a Syndicated (FOX) Type affiliate or a Sponsored Propaganda Channel that had unlimited permission to Distribute "FAKE ADS" attempting to Elect Or Recently Reelect the Former President.

## SOCIAL MEDIA AND TIK-TOK "CORPORATE"
# BUILD-A-BRAIN
### TAKEOVER Has to be STOPPED...

And Now it seems that the (BIG-3) has (Seem-isly) Installed their Social Media Format both Sociably, Financially, and Now "Politically" with Various Technical Platforms into Our Society.  And to be perfectly "Blunt" and to (Now) describe "My Overall Personal Observation" of what Social Media felt like (TO ME), and what It has Literally (Done) to My immediate Family has been a Nightmare:

In terms of what I have Personally Experienced with My Family has been completely (And) Literally (Eye-Popping), with Over 75% or more of their time, seems to be Spent (Or) have been Refocused to an Extremely "Noticeable Self Isolation" that (Social Media) seems to have, literally put (Down), a Full (Deposit) on certain individuals in my Household, and have Provided and equipped them with, what seems to be a Full Fledged "Social Media Starter-Kit" And what's (Scarry), for the most part, is that they must have Randomly – "Rented Out their Entire "Brain" and (Quickly Re-Modeled) My Family's Entire Life with Social Media.

This alone, (As I Use My family for an Example) has caused my Family Members to be Completely away from Any, and (All) Normal engagements and Family Functions for Hours and Hours daily. My family seems to have allegedly "Snuck" and – Taken a Secret "Oath to a Social Media Algorithm" Almost Like if they had been put In a *"Digital Trance or a Artificial Allegiance"* as if they have surrendered and given their full support, that is mostly (Engaged and Focused) on Streams of (Untrue and Un-factual) Information that is received from Social Media News Feeds.

It's Now Correct to Say that (Mr. Louis Wirth) former President of the International Sociological Association was onto Something in (1938) On Social Media and the Potential Family (Isolation) in our Society.

And in My Case, It Seems that, If I could further (Describe) my Observation of my "Own Families" Sudden Change, and their individual Behavior, and Obvious Distraction, of how

Social Media has affected Me and (My) Own Family.

It appears (Almost - Jokingly) As If "Someone Had Hired" a Professional Anesthesiologist" That Somehow Enter into Our Home unannounced and, "Digitally & Intravenously" Injected an, **(Unknown Social Media, Type Of) "Digital Serum" And then (Jokingly) Placed on a "Strict Social Media Diet".**

And Now with that being said, my entire family's (Overall Action's and Functionality) has become almost "Unrecognizable": As if they have been Digitally "Compromised" Or (Tampered with), an Given a Unknown Addiction, from a (Insidious Algorithmic Virus) Without their Permission or even knowing how it even happened:

It has also been a (Noticeable Difference) on the way they "Think" and engage towards family, as well as Inner-Acting with others and their immediate family, when it comes to what and when they Eat, Sleep, and it also seem they have (Adopted) with a "Gig-Like" Work Habit, especially with the (Gen-X) Group, that appears to have Suddenly - Given up on (Any) Formal Degreed Education and (Or) Vocational Training (Simply Settling) for the (Quick-Cash) and Online "Non-Unionized" No-Benefits, No Tax or Social Security Structured Benefit (Type) of Jobs (JUST SO THAT THEY CAN WORK ALTERED JOB HOURS) ALLOWING THEM MORE TIME TO SPEND ON SOCIAL MEDIA.  They also seem to have either Abandoned or have no Interest in establishing a Reliable structured (401-k) type Skilled Job, that offers benefits along with a Retirement System Due to the Distractions from Social Media.

And "Sadly" - at the end-of the Day...

They Just May, End up Being, like the (Majority of Today's Younger Society) that's Under the "Spell Of Social Media" and Platforms like TIK-TOK, Along with their Digital Devices", Just May end up Being the "Best" (Employee of the Month) Driving for

UBER, DOORDASH, Or just being the Next One, that is "Literally Waiting in Line" Of becoming the Next "Overnight" Online YOUTUBE/TIK-TOK/ or even a INSTAGRAM MODEL/// Or, Or, Or... (A) "Content Creator/Influencer/Advisor/Keyboard Sensation". "Phew", Sorry did I miss any of them. LOL, Just Saying:(

I'm Just Saying, I have always told my Family that, I have Yet to See, "ANY (DAM) DIPLOMA, OR CERTIFICATE" From UBER, DOORDASH, YOUTUBE, INSTAGRAM, TIK-TOK, SNAPCHAT, INSTA-CART,
(O'h) I'm sorry, did I Mention TIK-TOK.

# L.A.T.T

## LIFE AFTER TIK-TOK

## TIK - TIK - TOK

# BOOOM!

**Sooo, do you have Any**
**Life After Tik-Tok**
**Plans?**
**YOU BETTER HURRY DOORS ARE SOON**
**CLOSING!**

**SPOILER ALERT TO THE DAILY SOCIAL**
**MEDIA USER:**

**TIC-TOK IS OWNED BY THE "BYTE DANCE"**
**CORPORATION, THAT IS ASSOCIATED WITH**
**AND PRESENTLY CONTROLLED BY**
**COMMUNIST CHINA, TIK-TOK HAS BEEN**
**GIVEN A WARNING TO DISBAND AND DIS-**
**ASSOCIATE THEIR TIES WITH CHINA OR**
**THEY WILL BE "BANNED" ON JANUARY 19,**
**2025:**

**SO, THIS IS FOR THE TIK-TOK HEADS,**
**YOU'VE BEEN OFFICIALLY WARNED:**

Nowadays with Social Media and their (Isolated) environment, it has been extremely (Impactful), especially on our Generation (X) and Our Young Adults. The average person spends (70-81%) of their Valuable time, that has been Visually (Locked-In) and continually distracted and completely Diminished with (Digital Isolation) on various Social Media Platforms, "Totally Infused and Confused" On, "TIK-TOK's Yummy (Mind-Numbing-Flavorless) Daily Refill".

They also appear to have become somewhat detached from their own Emotional Feelings, to (Selfishly) engage and to "Virtually CLOCK-IN" just like, if they were On a UnOfficial, and "Invisible Time Clock" just like being on a Regular (Job) For Over (12 + HOURS) a Day.

As they Spend time (Away) from a (Normal) Daily Schedule, or with their Immediate friends and family, they just rather spend time, And "Comfortability" of Belonging to a Group Chat (and or) just so that they can be Awarded Emotional Likes Of Frivolous Emojis from Strangers in their (preferred) and Isolated Groups...

Or "Just, to be Alone", away from Others in a (Dimmed) and "Coddled" Atmosphere with their Digital Device completely closed off "Happily" from others and Family Members, And Now, With their Self Abandonment, that seems to have become Normal to them to be completely Isolated.

And as I (Look Back), and to be Completely Honest, with Today's Social Media Technology (Such as) the New IPhone and Various Mobile Devices, it appears to Have COMPLETELY...I Repeat, Have COMPLETELY...

"Purchased My Entire Family" (One by One) As if they were (Bought and Sold) to the Highest "SOCIAL MEDIA BIDDER" For a Meger Cost of Only ($1,200 to $1,600) Dollar Purchase, Of the Latest, I-Phone or Android Device and a TIK-TOK Injected Algorithm, Or whatever the current Price is of the Newest and latest "Shiny Object" that can be attach to a Social Media Platform:

# That has Been Conveniently coupled (Algorithmically), and formatted to Every Social Media Platform and Mobile Device:

"Hell" if the (BIG-3) Corporations can continue to Turn, "BILLIONS INTO TRILLIONS" In Profits and Not be Regulated by the Government, Well, if that's the Case then, Who needs Friends and Family?

Today's average Social Media User is "Never, Ever" without Their Mobile Device, and are Always engaged In – (or) On Social Media...

Just like the Old "AMERICAN EXPRESS" CREDIT CARD COMMERCIAL", THEY NEVER LEAVE HOME WITHOUT (IT) THEIR PHONE.

And with the Introduction Of Social Media and the impact with "My Entire Family" has completely (Disappeared Unknowingly),

"RIGHT BEFORE MY EYES" (Both) Mentally, and Physically as well as Subliminally, *(With Me not even having the ability) to Detect, Defend or Recognize it, Or even know what Hit-me, Until It was too Late...*

And Now I strongly Believe that the "GREEDY-3" actually knew the "BEGINNING, THE MIDDLE, AND THE END" of all the Mental and Psychological Effects that may eventually Occur from the Usage of Social Media.

The Big-3 appears to have been given a "Technical Blueprint" as well as a descriptive (Design), and the "Green-Light", to Build a Sophisticated and Elaborate Platform, and a Social Network Grid, that has allowed them to use the Best (Digitized) "Technical Vessel" that Money could Buy, that has allowed them To Build the (GREEDY-3'S) Elaborate Social Media Platforms,That seems to have Rewired and has "Harnessed" all of our "Thoughts, Our Needs, and will slowly begin to eliminate all our Technical Human Functions along with our Traditional Family Values" just by –

"Swiping a Password" or logging into a Digital Device that will have complete Access AND CONTROL of your entire Families (Past, Present, and Future) of their Entire life's History.

Please Note: This Historical data was used for Reference Purposes Only and was also used as a personal opinion of value, and to (By-Pass) the "Trolls"

At this point we also have to look at the emotional impact that has (Altered) the way people socialize with each other, that has Simply, (For the most Part) has completely and digitally "Checked Out" From Your entire Family, and their regular daily activities. Social Media has (Conveniently) replaced your entire Family with their "New (FAKE) Isolated Social Media Family and Friends...

*And* Now, with their *(New* Social Media Family) in Place, on the (Pre-Designed) Social Media Platforms and Algorithms, has basically allowed them to (Hurdle) over Regular

Communication and structured Family and Friends Relationships.

I "Honestly" believe that the Plan for Social Media Has Been in the Pre-Developmental Stage for Years and Years, Just like various Technology prior to their Releasing it to the General Public like the Microwave, and the VCR, knowingly that eventually Everybody would have access to One. And Now (Just) Like the Digital Devices and Phones, with the Unlimited access to Social Media.

And it appears to have *"Untraditionally"* ... *And "Contiguously" have* Detached the Casual everyday User (One -by One) from their Regular Daily activities and "Algorithmically" inserted a Corporate "Mindset" with the Social Media Agenda.

L.A.T.T   LIFE AFTER TIK-TOK

## QUESTION:

HAS THE SOCIAL MEDIA CORPORATIONS LIKE TIK-TOK BEEN ALLOWED TO CHANGE

OUR LIVES AND OUR FAMILY AND HAVE TAKEN US TO A POINT OF NO RETURN?

And What also appears what the various Platform's, has done was a Complete "SETUP", almost as if the (BIG-3's) Social Media's Group did, was,that they held a "Silent Auction" (Unconscionably) On the American Public, that appears to have "Re-Attached" the Everyday Social Media (User's) and "Funneled" them directly to the GREEDY-3's, UN-REGULATED "Algorithmic Corporate TRAP", and it is believed that this was (allegedly) done By design. For the Ultimate "MONEY GRAB", that's worth Billions.

That has Created this Social Media "Craze" that has given the Everyday Social Media User, a "Unidentified", Unregulated "SOCIAL MEDIA ROAD MAP" That Seems to Have been given Directions from a (Pre-Programed GPS) Directly to the (BIG-3's) New Corporate Office @ "BUILD-A-BRAIN" ...

Designed just for their Daily Social Media (12 + Hour Scrolling Session), as they Endless Scroll Amongst their (Like Minded) Random Social Media users that they Now Call their New Friends and Family...

# CHAPTER FOUR:
## WE GOT THE RECEIPTS

HOW MUCH DO SOCIAL MEDIA ACTUALLY SPEND ON SOCIAL MEDIA (VS) MONEY SPENT ON MEDICAL RESEARCH AND THE EFFECTS FROM ITS USE, HAS NOT BEEN ANSWERED:

Yes, we have the Receipts and the "Proof" And a Basic Breakdown on how much Social Media do Companies actually Spend on (Research & Development) VS: (Money spent for Research) from the Effects Of Social Media.

Companies Like Google spend Billions just on research and development in the amount of ($45 Billion) In development and New Technology.  As well as (Facebook) have dedicated and spent a substantial portion of their budget to (R & D), Just On the advancement involving algorithms alone, they also are in the  user interface, artificial intelligence, and data analysis used on their social media platforms, But doesn't seem to provide information or Budget on how much is spent towards Physical or the Mental effects from Social Media.

And Even Smaller Social Media Companies may spend considerably less, with figures ranging from hundreds of millions to a few billion dollars depending on their size and ambitions.

Here are some key points to consider. In what, the BIG-3 also spends Millions on Washington (Lobbyists) and Local State and Federal Politicians to Pass Laws...

For Example, here is a recent article from the (Associated Press): Politics Aug 31, 2023, 8:33 PM EDT: NEWS PBS.ORG

Judge blocks Arkansas law requiring parental approval for minors to create social media accounts:

LITTLE ROCK, Ark. (AP) — A federal judge on Thursday temporarily blocked Arkansas from enforcing a new law that would have required parental consent for minors to create new social media accounts, preventing the state from becoming the first to impose such a restriction.

U.S. District Judge Timothy L. Brooks granted a preliminary injunction that NetChoice — a tech industry trade group whose members include TikTok, Facebook parent Meta, and X, formerly known as Twitter — had requested against the law. The measure, which Republican Gov. Sarah Huckabee Sanders signed into law in April, was set to take effect Friday.

Arkansas' law is similar to a first-in-the-nation restriction signed into law earlier this year in Utah. That law is not set to take effect until March 2024. NetChoice last year filed a lawsuit challenging a California law requiring tech companies to put kids' safety first by barring them from profiling children or using personal information in ways that could harm children physically or mentally.

In a 50-page ruling, Brooks said NetChoice was likely to succeed in its challenge to the Arkansas law's constitutionality and questioned the effectiveness of the restrictions. END

And to also include an additional Article of what Social Media spends on R&D Is Staggering In Comparison to what they Spend on Research on the effects and Impact that

Social Media Spend further explains that it is (Minimal to (Non) Existence):

For (Example): Of a recent 2024 Article from (Statista) stated that the R&D costs of online companies that were spent in 2023 were in the Billions.

Statista, Reported the Following Article: Internet companies: research and development expenditure 2023...

During the most recent year, (Alphabet Google) spent over 45 billion... Companies like Alphabet (Google) and Meta (Facebook) dedicate substantial portions of their budget to R&D, including advancements in algorithms, user interface, artificial intelligence, and data analysis used on their social media platforms. Varied spending based on scale: Smaller social media companies may have smaller R&D budgets, focusing on core features and maintenance rather than large-scale innovation.

Factors affecting R&D cost: The complexity of features, platform development, and the need for constant updates can all contribute to the overall R&D spending on social media.

R&D costs of online companies 2023 - Statista To give you a brief idea, the cost to build a social media app can vary from $30,000 to $250,000, depending on various elements…

And Believe it or Not, here is Recent (INFORMATION) on what is Spent on Medical Research on the Effects from Social Media, and What the (BIG-3's) Contribution and Budget that's in Place. *AND IT APPEARS THAT THIS INFORMATION ON HOW MUCH THEIR BUDGET THAT IS SPENT TOWARDS (MEDICAL RESEARCH AND THE EFFECTS IT APPEARS THAT INFORMATION IS NOT CLEARLY AVAILABLE.*

AND HERE IS THE RESPONSE THAT I RECEIVED AFTER MAKING SEVERAL ATTEMPTS TO SEE WHAT WAS THE BUDGET FROM SOCIAL MEDIA COMPANIES ON THE BASIC QUESTION ON (MEDICAL RESEARCH) … AND HOW MUCH OF YOUR BUDGET IS

SET ASIDE FOR (MEDICAL RESEARCH) ON SOCIAL MEDIA?

STANDARD CORPORATE RESPONSE: While the exact amount Google spends on research to examine the effects of social media is not (Publicly disclosed), it's likely a significant portion of their overall research and development budget, with experts speculating it could be in the millions of dollars annually, as social media plays a major role in their advertising strategy and user behavior understanding.

And Once again another yet Random Response of what is spent on the Effects from the Social Media Corporations: While there is no readily available, publicly disclosed figure for the exact budget spent by top social media companies directly on research into the mental and physical effects of social media use, it's important to note that most companies do allocate some funding towards research in this area, though the exact amount is often considered "Proprietary Information" this research is usually incorporated into their broader efforts to understand user behavior and improve platform design, often including initiatives to promote positive user experiences and mitigate potential harms.

Typically, the marketing department within a company has the budget to examine the effects of social media, with the marketing manager or CMO overseeing the analysis and allocating funds for research and tracking tools to measure social media impact; however, depending on the organization's structure, other teams like data analysts or research departments may also contribute to this effort, especially when examining broader societal impacts.

IN CLOSING, IT'S SAFE TO SAY THAT I'M STILL CONFUSED, OF HOW MUCH (OR) IF ANY OF THEIR BUDGET IS SPENT ON THE EFFECTS AND MEDICAL RESEARCH FROM SOCIAL MEDIA.

Please Note: This Historical data was used for Reference Purposes Only that has Been Fact Checked, and is used as a personal opinion of value, and to (By-Pass the "Trolls"

THE TIK-TOK DOOR'S ARE "SOON" CLOSING... AMERICA CAN FINALLY GET BACK TO NORMAL FROM THE CLUTCHES OF SOCIAL MEDIA'S CORPORATE GREED, ALGORITHMS AND THEIR

## "BUILD-A-BRAIN"
### TAKEOVER

# L.A.T.T
### LIFE AFTER TIK-TOK

# CHAPTER FIVE:
## STOP THE "S.C.A.M.P"

"Social-Media, Corporate Algorithmic Media People"

YEAH! I SAID IT, And here's the reason why...

Here's the Deal, The (S.C.A.M.P) Acronym was created (By Me) IHaD Tu TELLuM while i was Putting Together this "Information Guide" And To bring a (Necessary) awareness to the potential problem towards the "Dis-Information" when it comes to Social Media.

As well as, to give a brief definition and the Awareness to the Social Media user and to also further (Attempt) to be a "Louder Voice" and to get the needed attention and information for the Everyday User.

And to also get answers from the S.C.A.M.P. Corporate PEOPLE, and to possibly begin a Mission to put a solution and Answer to the Question...

It Appears that the (BIG-3's) Budget is mostly Spent on (R&D) and further development of their Algorithms. That can eventually create echo chambers that have reinforced negative thought patterns and contribute to (A) Polarized Social Media Users Thinking.

And Below I was able to research the following Information and the effects from the Usages of Social Media. AND IF POSSIBLE, (PASS AND HIGHLIGHT THE INFORMATION BELOW AND SHARE)

Self-Esteem:

Platforms like Instagram can foster a culture of comparison that negatively impacts body image and self-esteem.

Misinformation:

Social media logic can lead to a distorted understanding of events and ideas by facilitating the rapid spread of information without sufficient verification.

Fringe views:

Algorithms can amplify fringe views and put them in the public discourse, which can lead to people organizing around them, and also with Age-inappropriate content, Unregulated and Unsupervised Algorithms can expose users to content that is far from age-appropriate, especially for children.

AND WHAT I (ALSO) THINK AT THIS POINT, IS THAT, THE (BIG-3'S), "SOCIAL MEDIA LICENSE" SHOULD BE "REVOKED": UNTIL FURTHER NOTICE, OR UNTIL THEY ARE ABLE TO FIGURE OUT, AS WELL AS BE (TRUTHFUL) TO THE AMERICAN PUBLIC OF THE POTENTIAL EFFECTS AND MEDICAL RESEARCH ON THE IMPACT FROM THE USAGE OF SOCIAL MEDIA, AND THEIR ANNUAL FUNDING. AND TO SUBMIT AN APPLICABLE WARNING LABEL BEFORE IT'S TO LATE...

However, algorithms also have some positive uses Such as:

Filtering:

> Algorithms can sort and match content to audiences with similar preferences, which can help users navigate through a flood of posts.

To minimize the harmful effects of social media, you can try limiting how much time you spend on it.  You can also create a plan with your child to limit social media, such as 30 minutes a day. AT THE END OF THE DAY, I BASICALLY CONCLUDED THAT...

It is Also Perceived that there is "No Dedicated Budget" for the Mental or Psychological Effects for the Usage of Social Media.  And that Most research and funding for social media effects is likely integrated within broader mental health research budgets, making it (Extremely) difficult to isolate the exact amount spent solely on social media studies.

Researchers and lawmakers have long focused on the negative effects stemming from social media platforms, whose personally tailored algorithms can drive children towards excessive use. Recently, lawmakers in states like New York and Utah introduced or passed legislation that would curb social media use among kids, citing harm to youth mental health and other concerns.

Here is some additional Information that I would like to give -a- (Shout Out) from (Tech Writer Brian X Chen), Brian's article and information that was extremely helpful that's available to read Online, that references the Impact from Technology Linking it to Loneliness.

Brian X. Chen

**How Technology and Loneliness are Interlinked**

Technology and loneliness are interlinked, researchers have found, stoked by the ways we interact with Social Media.

PLEASE NOTE: This data was used for Reference Purposes Only that has Been Fact Checked and is used as a personal opinion of value, and to also (By-Pass the "Trolls")

In Closing: I have provided a "Brief Snapshot" of How and when It All Began:

In the late 90s and early 2000s, when platforms like Six Degrees, Friendster, and MySpace were emerging, the potential harmful effects of overuse weren't as widely recognized or understood. However, some concerns were starting to surface:

Early Concerns "Ramped - Up" in the (Late 90s - Early 2000s):

Internet addiction: This was a broader concern, not specific to social media, but there were worries about people spending excessive time online, neglecting real-life responsibilities and relationships.

Privacy: People were starting to realize that sharing personal information online could have consequences, especially with the rise of cyberbullying and online predators.

Social isolation: There was some concern that online interaction might replace face-to-face communication, leading to social isolation and loneliness.

PLEASE NOTE: This information is Similar to the Research that I provided earlier from (Mr. Louis Wirth's) article that featured (social Isolation, from his (1938) Article, as well as the Article from Brian X Chen's recent Article, and the ARTICLE as Mentioned in the previous Chapter BY: KC Ifeanyi.

**Compared to Today's Social Media:**

Today, the harmful effects of social media overuse are much more widely discussed and researched. Here are some key differences:

- **Scale and pervasiveness:** Social media is now deeply integrated into our lives, with billions of users and platforms designed to be highly engaging and addictive.
- **Algorithms and echo chambers:** Sophisticated algorithms curate our feeds, potentially reinforcing existing beliefs and limiting exposure to diverse perspectives, leading to echo chambers and polarization.
- **Mental health impact:** There's growing evidence linking excessive social media use to anxiety, depression, body image issues, and low self-esteem, particularly among young people.
- **Spread of misinformation:** The rapid spread of misinformation and fake news on social media can have serious

consequences, impacting elections, public health, and social cohesion.

- Cyberbullying and online harassment: The anonymity and reach of social media can amplify the impact of cyberbullying and online harassment, causing significant emotional distress.

From the Unregulated platforms: (Is it too Late)?

The lack of robust regulation in the early days allowed social media platforms to grow rapidly with less oversight. Today, there's increasing pressure to hold platforms accountable for harmful content, data privacy, and the impact of their algorithms.

In conclusion, while some concerns about internet overuse and privacy existed in the early days of social media, the scale and complexity of the issues have grown significantly. Today, we face a wider range of challenges, including the impact of algorithms, mental health concerns, misinformation, and online harassment, highlighting the need for greater awareness, regulation, and responsible use of these powerful platforms.

So there, Now that you have (Read)the information "literally" from the Horse's Mouth, SOOO... After the TIK-TOK Ban on 01/19/2025 goes into effect, what will Be your Plans?

# CHAPTER SIX
## LIFE OF THE SCROLL-A-HOLICS

Here are (Two) additional articles that were Published: According to a study from the Harvard T.H. Chan School of Public Health: Social media companies made $11 billion in the U.S. Ad revenue from "Minors".
The researchers say the findings show a need for government regulation of social media since the companies that stand to make money from children who use their platforms have failed to meaningfully self-regulate.

They note such regulations, as well as greater transparency from tech companies, could help alleviate harm to youth mental health and curtail potentially harmful advertising practices that target children and adolescents.

To come up with the revenue figure, the researchers estimated the number of users under 18 on Facebook, Instagram, Snapchat, TikTok, X (formerly Twitter) and YouTube in 2022 based on population data from the U.S. Census and survey data from Common Sense Media and Pew Research.

They then used data from research firm eMarketer, now called Insider Intelligence, and Qustodio, a parental control app, to estimate each platform's U.S. Ad revenue in 2022 and the time children spent per day on each platform.

After that, the researchers said they built a simulation model using the data to estimate how much (Ad) Revenue the platforms earned from minors in the U.S.

Meta, which owns Instagram and Facebook, is also being sued by dozens of states for allegedly contributing to the mental health crisis.

Although social media platforms may claim that they can self-regulate their practices to reduce the harms to young people, they have yet to do so, and our study suggests they have overwhelming financial incentives to continue to delay taking meaningful steps to protect children," said Bryn Austin, a professor in the Department of Social and Behavioral Sciences at Harvard and a senior author on the study.
END:

And in a Separate Article From a 2020 Policy Paper from the, American Academy of Pediatrics said: The platforms themselves don't make public how much money they earn from minors.

Social media platforms are not the first to advertise to children, and parents and experts have long expressed concerns about marketing to kids online, on television and even in schools.  But online ads can be especially insidious because they can be targeted to children and because the line between Ads and the content kids seek out is often blurry.

Children are "uniquely vulnerable to the persuasive effects of advertising because of immature critical thinking skills and impulse inhibition."
END:

**SPOILER ALERT TO THE DAILY SOCIAL MEDIA USER:**

**TIC-TOK IS OWNED BY THE "BYTE DANCE" CORPORATION, THAT IS ASSOCIATED WITH AND PRESENTLY CONTROLLED BY COMMUNIST CHINA, TIK-TOK HAS BEEN GIVEN A WARNING TO DISBAND AND DIS-ASSOCIATE THEIR TIES WITH CHINA OR THEY WILL BE "BANNED" ON JANUARY 19, 2025:**

# L.A.T.T
## LIFE AFTER TIK-TOK

# CHAPTER SEVEN
## BLIND LEADING THE BLIND

**BLIND LEADING THE BLIND, ON HOW FOLLOWERS BELIEVE THE CONTENT CREATOR WITHOUT FACT CHECKING THE CONTENT CREATORS, OR EVEN THE PERSON THAT THEY ARE FOLLOWING:**

And if you take a moment there seem to have been a steady (Influx) of (Fake) Influncers, which Have Created a "Grab-The-Viewer and Run" Tactic, that has been (Overly) Used by fake influencers, along with a (Treasure-Trove of Bot's) to Create a Glamorous Lifestyle and Appearance and also a Popularity Status just to portray a look of "Believe-Ability" to their Followers.

I bet if you really get to know these people and their Overall personality, you may find out that most of these Influencers and followers are just as miserable internally as the ones who actually Look up to them, and Probably will actually have (Waaayy) more problems than you have.

And even Now it appears that Influencers (Can No - Longer) Even, Influence their Own audience, and are Unable to (Attract New Followers) along with the existing followers to even continue following the Actual (Original Content Creator that they are Following): As the average (Followers) eventually end -Up (Unsubscribing)  all together from their Channel and would eventually will just seek additional Entertainment and information from another Social Media Channel.

And again, there are various surveys that show that there is only a (3-5%) Traction Rate and (Sustainability) from (Today's followers) that are received from (Traditional influencers) that is actually, even considered to be of any (Value to the Influencer) in today's Social Media Market.

Even like the (Medium) to the Smaller (You-Tubers) and TIK-TOK's (Fav-Favorites) Content Creators like "Tasha - K's" Steady Climb Of Intelligent and "JUICY" and "Tantalizing" must Hear Gossip And Reaction Type of Content, (She and She alone), Has "Carved Out" a Great and Loyal Following; And Does Her "Fair Share" of Talking S#*t, and still has been able to provide "Fact-Checkable" content with a  "Hell-of-A-Tagline" along with Her "Wine Down" With

Tasha K and Her Brand Of "Wine-O's" and information, She has been able to present and support her consistently Followed Audience:

Even to give a "Shout-Out" to the "So-Called" (Up & Comers) like Dwayne & Jazz, Or Jay & Sasha Song,  and with the most (Recently) addition to the Roster, with the so-called "New Kid on the Block" (Mr. Shannon Sharpe's) who has Suddenly had a "BOOM-BOOM-ZOOOM EFFECT" Of Factual Content, that has been (Simply Phenomenal) as well as His (Non-bashfulness) in Picking his Guest with some of the Best, like a KATT WILLIAMS, or a KEVIN HART, just To name a few. And who would have Known Shannon Sharp's Hidden talent, and His "ABBRA-CA-DABBRA Azzz Move, especially after he finally left "Skip"

And to set the Record straight and to "Keep - It 100%" and if you have a (Channel or are (Ambition-ally) Seeking (Talent) to start a Channel On Social Media, You should Strongly Consider, Providing Relevant and Creative (Content) "I REPEAT Creative Content" towards your Platform audience. And if YOU Have a Somewhat engaginging (Personality) that can accumulate a Loyal Following... (And if this is the Case), Then you just May have a Shot, and Should be able to grow your Channel Successfully.

But if you have a Celebrity following, like a Taylor Swift, a Beyonce, or an Oprah Winfrey, with that type of Insane following and Influence... Well then, the Sky's the Limit.

And With that type of Influential Voice on Social Media Like that, could be an extreme (focus) and a possible conversation of the Importance that can be used towards the impact and effects of Social Media.

## L.A.T.T.

### LIFE AFTER TIK-TOK

THE TIK-TOK DOOR'S ARE "SOON" CLOSING... AMERICA CAN FINALLY GET BACK TO NORMAL, FROM THE CLUTCHES OF SOCIAL MEDIA'S CORPORATE ALGORITHMS, GREED, AND THEIR

# "BUILD-A-BRAIN

## SOCIAL MEDIA

### TAKEOVER

# CHAPTER EIGHT
## A SPECIAL TRIBUTE:

Yes, I titled this chapter, (A SPECIAL TRIBUTE) Because I wanted to give (KC Ifeanyi) a Personal Thank-you, And that's because after reading (KC's) Article (Below) Was extremely Accurate and truthful, That seem to have a "Special Ingredient" is what I got from the Article. And this particular research is what Inspired me to put this (Informational Guide) together and for Me to Go, into a further (Retrieval) of FACTUAL INTELLIGENCE, and Information that has "Contiguously" built a Social Media Bridge into a larger platform and to also help and provide further information and awareness of the unrestricted Case study of the (GOOD THE BAD AND THE UGLY) "Corporate Algorithms" and the impact and effects from the use of Social Media that I personally experienced from gathering this information from this article, for my own family:

Respectfully,

IHaD Tu TELLuM

## ARTICLE BY:

## KC Ifeanyi

# Inside the good, bad, and very ugly of social media algorithms

There's a lot to unpack with the current state of social media algorithms. Fast Company's podcast Creative Conversation explored this topic: BY KC Ifeanyi

It feels strange to think back to a time when we weren't so concerned with social media algorithms. To the layperson, algorithms were just a nebulous mix of code that we knew controlled what we were seeing in our feeds, but most of us weren't bothered. We accepted the idea that they were a good thing serving us more of what we love. That's true—to a certain point.

The 2016 presidential election and the fallout from the <u>Cambridge Analytica scandal</u> was a tipping point in how we think about what pops up in our feeds, as well as the offline ramifications of social media echo chambers.

Those blinkered content streams only rushed more furiously that same year, as Instagram and Twitter took a cue from Facebook's News Feed and switched to algorithmically ranked feeds as well. Since then, social media algorithms have been under increasing scrutiny.

Ex-Google engineer Guillaume Chaslot <u>criticized YouTube's recommendation engine</u> for promoting conspiracy theories and divisive content. The documentary *<u>The Social Dilemma</u>* <u>was a buzzy exposé</u> of how these platforms manipulate human behavior. Tik Tok enigmatic For You page was called out for suppressing videos from disabled creators in a bid to mitigate bullying and harassment (a policy the company says is no (longer in place). Most recently, former Facebook data scientist turned whistleblower <u>Frances Haugen released thousands of internal documents</u> showing what Facebook and Instagram executives knew about the potential harms of their platforms.

In short, there's a lot to unpack in the current state of play with social media algorithms. Covering what we know (but more specifically what we don't know) about how these algorithms work, their toll on our mental health, and what effective government regulation should look like.

### The "black box" problem
What we know of how social media algorithms work often feels dwarfed by how much we don't know, which Kelley Cotter, an assistant professor in the College of Information

Sciences and Technology at Penn State University, frames as "the black box problem."

Cotter asserts that companies are intentionally opaque with how their algorithms work to protect proprietary tech and avoid any potential scrutiny. Social media platforms have given cursory explanations of why certain content winds up in your feed, albeit exactly what you'd expect: Videos or photos that have high engagement—comments, likes, shares, and so forth—are more likely to bubble to the surface. But, to Cotter, those explanations amount to little more than PR moves.

"A lot of it also, is made up of rationales," Cotter says. "So not just, 'This is what the algorithm does,' but 'It does this because we want X to happen.' Usually it's like, 'We want to make sure that you're seeing the things that you care about or you're making real connections with people.' So, it's really a lot of couching of the information in these really lofty goals that they have." What is clear about social media algorithms is that Tik Tok has become the one to reckon with.

In Meta's first quarter earnings call, CEO Mark Zuckerberg announced Facebook's and Instagram feeds would incorporate more content from accounts users they don't follow but that they may find interesting. It's an obvious attempt to be in better competition with TikTok's popular For Your page, an endless scroll of discoverability that's been a major factor in the platform's growth—as well as a source of mystery. The general consensus on TikTok's algorithm is that it's *too* good.

Since TikTok boomed into the zeitgeist during the pandemic, Creators and users alike have been trying to crack what makes the all-important (For You Page) so adept at predicting which videos will resonate.

*The New York Times* obtained verified documents from TikTok's engineering team in Beijing that explained to non-technical employees how the algorithm works. A computer scientist who reviewed the documents for the *Times* said TikTok's recommendation engine is "totally reasonable, but traditional stuff," and that the platform's advantage is in the massive volumes of data and a format structured for recommended content.

Software engineer Felecia Coleman would agree—to a point. Coleman is one of many creators who have tried to hack Tik-Tok's algorithm. Through her experimentation, Coleman posits that Tik-Tok has a "milestone mechanism" (i.e., a point where the algorithm boosts your content when you reach a certain number of videos), as well as a prioritization structure (e.g., front-loading content from what the algorithm deems to be Black Creators during Black History Month or Juneteenth.  Those are fairly intuitive findings that took her from about 4,400 followers when she started her experiment to 170,000 in a month.

But Coleman recognizes there are still anomalies in Tik-Tok's algorithms that may not yield similar results for other creators. "They have a lot of room for improvement when it comes to being more transparent about why certain content is reported, why certain content is blocked, because a lot of people have no choice but to assume that they have been shadow banned," Coleman says. "As an engineer, I can understand that might not be the case under the hood. There might just be an algorithm that's getting something wrong.

But we need to let the users know that, because there are really emotional and psychological effects that happen to people when they're left in the dark."

## An Algorithmic Addiction

Social media algorithms are designed with retention in mind: The more dedicated eyeballs, the more advertising revenue that pours in. For some people, scrolling through social media for hours on end mainly leaves them feeling guilty for having wasted a chunk of their day. But for others, getting sucked in like that can have a major impact on their mental health. Studies have shown that high levels of social media use have been linked to increased depression and anxiety in both teens and adults. It's something Dr. Nina Vasan has seen firsthand as a psychiatrist— and something she's trying to help social media platforms mitigate through her work as the founder of Brainstorm, Stanford's academic lab focusing on mental health innovation.

For example, Brainstorm worked with Pinterest to create a "<u>compassionate search</u>" experience where if users searched for topics such as quotes about stress or work anxiety, there would be guided activities to help improve their mood. Vasan and her team also worked with Pinterest's engineers to prevent potentially harmful or triggering content from auto filling in search or being recommended.

One of the most important issues that Vasan is trying to solve across the board is breaking the habit of endless (and mindless) scrolling on social media. The algorithms have developed with the intention of keeping us online. The problem is that there's no ability to pause and think. Time just basically goes away," Vasan says. "We need to think about how we can break the cycle and look at something else, take a breath."

Platforms, including TikTok and Instagram, have introduced features for users to monitor how much time they're spending in the apps. But Louis Barclay had a more radical solution for breaking his Facebook addiction that <u>subsequently got him banned</u>.

Around six years ago, Barclay started noticing just how much time he and everyone else around him was spending online. So, he quit his job in investment banking, taught himself how to code, and started creating to help reduce our addiction to the internet. One of those tools was Unfollow Everything, a browser extension that essentially allowed Facebook users to delete their News Feeds by unfollowing friends, groups, and pages. Unfollowing is a function Facebook launched in 2013 that lets users unfollow but not unfriend the people they're connected to.

Only Barclay created a way to do it automatically and on a scale. "I am the first person to say that I'm not anti every single thing that Facebook or Instagram does. But at the same time, the fact that you have to go via this addictive central heart, this feed, to get to those other useful things, to go into that amazing support group that exists or talk to your grandmother, that's the thing that really sucks for me, Barclay says. "So, I did feel this incredible sense of control from getting to decide what that default was gonna be."

However, Unfollow Everything violated Meta's terms of service, and Barclay was banned from both Facebook and Instagram. A Meta spokesperson tells *Fast Company* that both platforms have been implementing tools that give users more control over what they see in their feeds.

The spokesperson also mentions that the company has reached out to Barclay multiple times this year to resolve the issue of him being banned. So, If or when Barclay gets back on these platforms remains to be seen. But his focus at the moment is researching and inventing more ways for users to have a healthier relationship with social media through his latest project, Nudge, a Chrome extension to help people spend less time on the internet, as well as working with researchers to understand better what more can be done in this area.

"One of the first things that we need to do to be able to regulate against big tech is to get solid research showing which kind of interventions we should actually put into law," Barclay says.
END:

# CHAPTER NINE
## AND THE EXPERTS - SAY'S!!! THE SOCIAL MEDIA'S PROOF IS DEFENTANLY IN THE PUDDING:

Yes, at this Point, so far, the research data that has been provided in this (Informational Guide) has been from my personal

experiences, and from what I have observed from my own family's perspective. This particular research has been fact checked, and chosen from various articles, just so I will be able to (Conclude) and to have a somewhat understanding of the effects from Social Media.

### AND I CAN'T WAIT TO TASTE THIS DAM' PUDDING:

Just so that I could further study the effects from the Usage of Social Media. Due to the Lack of (Knowledge and Information) that Appears to be unavailable.

And What is also Baffling, and Interesting is the fact that the (BIG-3) has Spent (Billions and Billions) of Dollars as mentioned in (Previous) Chapters, Just on Research and Development R&D, and has Spent "Dam-Near"

(Zero Dollars) on Research of the Effects from Social Media:

So here are several Topics that you can (Fact Check Yourself) on this particular Subject, That List some of the effects that may occur from the Usage of Social Media.

Here's a Brief List and Perspective such as:

#1. The Effects from Filter Bubbles, In which will Explain how algorithms create filter bubbles, exposing us to limited perspectives and potentially reinforcing biases.

#2. Addiction and The release of Dopamine, that further Explains and Explores the addictive nature of social media and how it triggers Dopamine releases, keeping users hooked.

#3. There has also been an "Up-Tick" on searching for Mental Health and to be further informed and to start a Discussion of the potential negative impacts of social media on mental health, including anxiety, depression, and low self-esteem.

And as I discussed in the Previous Chapter on my (Self-Made Definition) The S.C.A.M.P. People: SOCIAL MEDIA CORPORATE ALGORITHM MEDIA PEOPLE.

And the focus on Strategies for (Managing Brain Overload), That will allow yourself to use more Mindful Consumption as well as to Encourage Social Media Users to be more aware of their social media use, and to set limits and be aware and selective about the content that you consume.

#5. You should Also learn or get information on how to begin a (Digital Detox) and allow yourself to take breaks and disengage from social media and reconnect with Your immediate Family and Friends, and away from your daily online Social Media regiment.

#6. And if you are not familiar with information and resources on information and courses on (Critical Thinking) and how to include it in your daily life, can help emphasize the importance of questioning the information presented to you and individuals that you are associated with on social media.

#7. And it is also Important to (Grasp) and understand how (Algorithms can actually affect you) by educating yourself on how Algorithms work, and how they can influence your online experiences.

#8. By exploring these Several topics and aspects of how to Navigate through the (S.C.A.M.P. People), that was discussed in (Chapter Five). If possible, to use topics that were just mentioned (1 - through 7) in your Daily Life, this will hopefully help you. Filter through some Companies online, I even found a great Company "like (WONDERMIND.COM) that Seems to have valuable information on how to avoid various pitfalls as well as help the chances of you restoring valuable insights into the impact of Social Media, that may can possibly provide or begin to offer practical strategies for navigating your ups and downs from the usage of Social Media in a healthy and mindful way and to always engage and practice Mindful Social Media Consumption to help reduce possible Brain Overload:

Please note to the Reader: That i have 'NO' Financial association with any of the Companies (Or) from any of the Articles that have been mentioned within this Information guide:

THE TIK-TOK DOOR'S ARE "SOON" CLOSING...
AMERICA CAN FINALLY GET BACK TO NORMAL FROM THE CLUTCHES OF SOCIAL MEDIA'S CORPORATE ALGORITHMS, GREED AND THEIR

# "BUILD-A-BRAIN"

TAKEOVER

# CHAPTER TEN

## THE "TIK-TOK" DOORS ARE NOW CLOSING...

Yes, this is another Warning TIk-TOK Will be Disbanded as of January 19, 2025, and this is why I began this Journey and wrote this (Information Guide), And why I came up with the Title L.A.T.T. LIFE AFTER TIK-TOK.

And the only thing that came to Mind, as I got towards the end of the Book, was a (1970's Classic) Hit...

### I Will Survive

### Song by Gloria Gaynor

The question is will "You Survive", or will you be able to withstand the withdrawal from the Absence of the TIK-TOK Platform? This book is about how individuals and families have unintentionally, both mentally and physically, checked out. We've become emotionally detached from real friends and family, replaced by an "Artificial Refill" of random social media users, thanks to a corporate algorithm. Let's be honest. Various corporations have focused on the everyday user of platforms like Instagram, TikTok, and Facebook. They've ignored the addictive nature of these platforms, especially for our youth. Ok, so at this point, Let's just (PAUSE) and try to sum things up…

And let's just Say, based on the Information within this Guide alone:  IN THAT IT APPEARS, THAT THE SOCIAL MEDIA CORPORATION LIKE FACEBOOK, YOUTUBE, (X) FORMERLY TWITTER, INSTAGRAM, TIK-TOK ALONG WITH THEIR SOPHISTICATED ALGORITHMS HAS PLAYED US…

Yup' We Got Played! LIKE A "CHEAP" GAME OF "THREE CARD MONTE CARD GAME"  Tik-Tok and Social Media has literally made Billions…It feels like, Social Media and TIK-TOK has Used Us like an "Outdated Expired Loaf of Bread" that has Put us on the Discount Sales Rack, (For Sale) with a Reduced priced at 90% Off: This was allowed with the Permission of Our Federal Government's Lack of Restriction:

And (NOW) if you look at the Social Media Corporations, while they ignored the Possible Alarming Effects both Mentally and Psychologically on today's Society, They

Have (Yet) to answer their Lack of Restriction. Along with "TIK - TOK's" (Handcuffed and) "Cozy Communist Affiliation with "BYTE DANCE".

There has not been a notable response to the Budget Amount Request for the actual cost of their (T.O.E) TOTAL OPERATIONAL EXPENSE", Into what has been Spent, (If any) Towards their Unfiltered Algorithms or its Potential Harms to our society.

Or what's the United States Plan that they have in Place to respond to Societies Questions of the Real Concerns about the Potential Societal shifts that could occur (Once) TikTok were to suddenly disappear. The American Society should be further appalled by the Non-Response along with the (Silence) from the Unregulated – Addictiveness, and (the) Ignored (Over - Tweaked Algorithms) and Videos from TIK-TOK'S "CASH-COW" Of Unmonitored Content that Millions received from TIK-TOK on a Daily

Basis, and what would the (Content Creators) and their Audience do Once it's gone?

It seems that all this was (Allegedly) Overlooked "Due to the (Lack) of regulations, and Monitoring of the (Byte Dance) corporation from the beginning. And their Blatant Non-Response and the Lack of any Laws that was (NEVER) Enforced. And have Allegedly led us to a Possible (addiction) of endless scrolling or may have left us damaged (Internally). That may have created an emotional void that may have led Millions of us Social Media Tik-Tok Users "Un – Rehabable"

Or may just result in and Place Our (Platforms and Businesses) in a Catastrophic Situation that may just result in Financial Ruins, with a lost that will be Irretrievable:

And how will that actually Look and how will you avoid the SOUND FROM THE "BIG-THUD" FROM THE TIK-TOK BAND?

How will we be able to handle the damage and take steps to mitigate Life After TikTok would be a Complete (Wake-up call). And now It's time to examine how we've been manipulated, and the consequences that we will face along with our well-being, and what life could be like if we can finally reclaim our time, attention and authentic connections with Life After Tik - Tok.

In closing to the (Social Media) Users, at the End Of the Day - We first must address The Immediate Aftermath and hopefully be able to Fully Recover and try to return to Normal Life functions, with a working formula of your Social Media Consumption for the most part, and I hope and Pray that the Average Social Media (Person(s) has already prepared a safe and reliable and financially;
"Strong and Secure Financial "Backup Plan"

I strongly believe that the Immediate Aftermath from the Sudden Absence of the "TIK-TOK" BAN, will affect people differently and will probably have, and may fill a sense of

Loss. That may Cause a mild Depression, for most of Us, that may also have a Psychological and Emotional Effect from having and relying on TIK-TOK as their Primary Source for Financial Purposes, Entertainment as well as a form of Withdrawals with lack of communication with Friends and Family, Or just plan end up being "Pissed Off" Once the Platform has been Dissolved:(

That's why it's important to have a structured plan in place for (L.A.T.T.) Life After Tik-Tok. That can Possibly assist you with the temporary Void that you may be experiencing as you re-adjust and restructure your Short Engaging Videos to a Long streaming Video especially if you are a Content Creator.  Or just decide to maybe just move to another platform to seek Entertainment Value.

I believe that a group of People including some Content Creators may not make any plans, and that they just don't believe that it won't even happen.  And will Probably wake up the next day, with a  Devastating and a Tremendous TIK-TOK "Social Media Hangover".

Once TIK-TOK is Banned and goes into Effect they will be Caught-up in The "Mad Scramble" for Alternatives. With the rush and Confusion and (Hectic) Decision Making will be enormously difficult to manage and to fill the gap or be left with skepticism of being reacquainted with the Older Apps and Platforms, or feel the Shakiness of the New and  Emerging Start -Up's - and Newcomers and their Platforms.

## Financial Impacts:

The Financial Impacts may affect the Creators and Influencers, "To a Point of No Return" and most will receive unknown challenges for the ones that have relied on TikTok for income must be able to adapt successfully and be able to merge a seamless transition to other platforms, and a new form of Income without any complication, and hopefully avoid any financial hardship, or just simply be forced to return back to Reality and "Tuck their Tail Between their Legs" and get a Normal and Dreadful (9 to 5). And for the ones that dont remember what that (Actually) would Look Like, it is Simply called, a JOB. And if you do, get one, try and get a JOB with some Benefits:

Social Media Content Providers will Have to also rebuild relationships that relied on TikTok for marketing and advertising and will have to readjust their overall strategies.

And Please keep this in mind to always DREAM SUCCESSFULLY...

# L.A.T.T.

## LIFE AFTER TIK-TOK

THE TIK-TOK DOOR'S ARE "SOON" CLOSING... AMERICA CAN FINALLY "GET BACK TO NORMAL" FROM THE CLUTCHES OF TIK-TOK AND SOCIAL MEDIA, AND ALL THE CORPORATE ALGORITHMS FROM

# TIK-TOK's
# "BUILD-A-BRAIN"
## SOCIAL MEDIA
## AND TIK-TOK TAKEOVER

TIC-TOK IS OWNED BY THE "BYTE DANCE" CORPORATION, THAT IS ASSOCIATED WITH, AND PRESENTLY CONTROLLED BY COMMUNIST CHINA, TIK-TOK HAS BEEN GIVEN A WARNING TO DISBAND AND DIS-ASSOCIATE THEIR TIES WITH CHINA OR THEY WILL BE "BANNED" ON JANUARY 19, 2025:

Again Thank-you and continue to (Fact Check) all your information and get the truth for you and your family and try to have a Nice and "Back to Normal Day" :)

## Written By

## IHaD TU TELLuM

# References Research and Factual Information Referenced by The following:)

Mr. Louis Wirth Information from (1938) Article

Special Support and Inspiration from,
KC Ifeanyi

M.O.B
MY-OWN-BRAIN
AND NOT FROM HERE-SAY,
TROLLS, FAKE-NEWS, OR BOT'S

Google/Fact Checked

Brian X Chen

Ap: Associated Press

PBS.ORG

STATISTA

PETER V. MARSDEN

SAMEER B. SRIVASTAVA

BRIAN SCHWALB (QUOTE)

AMERICAN ACADEMY OF
PEDIATRIC (POLICY PAPER)

TROMBLE & JOSHUA TUCKER (NYU)

McPHERSON, SMITH LOVIN
AND BRASHEARS

ARTHUR KORHAUSER (1968)

(MYSPACE, SIX DEGREES, FRIENDSTER)

MY OWN FAMILY AND FRIENDS
AND BELIEVE IT OR NOT
THEY USED THEIR OWN BRAINS:)

# L.A.T.T.

## LIFE AFTER TIK-TOK

**THE TIK-TOK DOOR'S ARE "SOON" CLOSING...
AMERICA CAN FINALLY GET BACK TO
NORMAL, FROM THE CLUTCHES OF SOCIAL
MEDIA'S CORPORATE ALGORITHMS, GREED,
AND THEIR**

## "BUILD-A-BRAIN - TAKEOVER"

**AND TRY TO HAVE A GREAT BACK TOO
NORMAL DAY...**

www.ingramcontent.com/pod-product-compliance
Lightning Source LLC
LaVergne TN
LVHW052302060326
832902LV00021B/3680